More Animal than Human
Mary A. Rogers

Indie Blu(e) Publishing
Havertown, Pennsylvania

Praise for *More Animal than Human*

"Transfixed by Mary's unbridled words, I found myself catching my breath as the poems opened me to long forgotten memories. Mary's poetry evokes the wilderness, the flight of Baba Yaga, and raw, human emotions; relatable, honest words that scrape the underworld of the soul. This is a collection you can return to over and over, poems for months like September, November, and any day where you long to dip into the mystic. I have long loved the integrity of Mary's word witchery - it excavates the things many have struggled with and risen from."

—Monika Carless, *Transforming the Mother Wound* and *The Dark Pool Trilogy*

"In her debut collection, *More Animal Than Human*, Mary A. Rogers has crafted a spell to heal a lifetime of anguish and abandonment, through the incantations of her poetry. These poems are accessible, open to all who journey on a path to spiritual reclamation, building a fire around the ever-blooming soul. She writes, "that night i slept/ in the belly of a whale/ i touched the edge/ of infinity/ i wept as i beheld/ the ineffable beauty/ flesh, tears, heartbeat/ soul salt and bone/ holy whore, made mother/ fallen angel, turned crone." This wolf-song book of wild reckoning swerves from the darkness of grief, to a respite in the quiet forest of trees, to a phoenix goddess becoming whole. "i watched her transform. her eyes lit with desire and feather by feather—she grew wings and caught fire." From the ashes, Mary's words light the way back to herself."

-Kai Coggin, author of *Mother of Other Kingdoms* and *Mining for Stardust*

"Ever the healer and the mystic, Mary has brought her true spirit to these pages. The verses of each rhythmic compilation showcase just how she feels the natural forces working within her. Much like the great balladeers of the wild world, Mary has created a collection of poetic anthems that speak volumes about her sensitivities and emotions within life itself. Such an excellent masterpiece that needs to be celebrated!"

-Gerry Ellen, *A Big Piece of Driftwood*

More Animal than Human
Mary A. Rogers, 2025
All rights reserved.

Printed in the United States of America.

No part of this book may be used, stored in a system retrieval system, or transmitted, in any form or in any means by electronic, mechanical, photocopying, recording or reproduced in any manner whatsoever without written permission from the publisher, except in the case of brief quotations embodied in critical articles and reviews.

For information, address
Indie Blu(e) Publishing
indieblucollective@gmail.com

Paperback ISBN: 978-1-951724-26-9
eBook ISBN: 978-1-951724-27-6
Library of Congress Control Number: 2024952265
Indie Blu(e) Editorial Team
Candice Louisa Daquin
Victoria Manzi
Christine E. Ray
Elijah R. Carney

Praise for *More Animal than Human*

"Transfixed by Mary's unbridled words, I found myself catching my breath as the poems opened me to long forgotten memories. Mary's poetry evokes the wilderness, the flight of Baba Yaga, and raw, human emotions; relatable, honest words that scrape the underworld of the soul. This is a collection you can return to over and over, poems for months like September, November, and any day where you long to dip into the mystic. I have long loved the integrity of Mary's word witchery - it excavates the things many have struggled with and risen from."

—Monika Carless, *Transforming the Mother Wound* and *The Dark Pool Trilogy*

"In her debut collection, *More Animal Than Human*, Mary A. Rogers has crafted a spell to heal a lifetime of anguish and abandonment, through the incantations of her poetry. These poems are accessible, open to all who journey on a path to spiritual reclamation, building a fire around the ever-blooming soul. She writes, "that night i slept/ in the belly of a whale/ i touched the edge/ of infinity/ i wept as i beheld/ the ineffable beauty/ flesh, tears, heartbeat/ soul salt and bone/ holy whore, made mother/ fallen angel, turned crone." This wolf-song book of wild reckoning swerves from the darkness of grief, to a respite in the quiet forest of trees, to a phoenix goddess becoming whole. "i watched her transform. her eyes lit with desire and feather by feather—she grew wings and caught fire." From the ashes, Mary's words light the way back to herself."

-Kai Coggin, author of *Mother of Other Kingdoms* and *Mining for Stardust*

"Ever the healer and the mystic, Mary has brought her true spirit to these pages. The verses of each rhythmic compilation showcase just how she feels the natural forces working within her. Much like the great balladeers of the wild world, Mary has created a collection of poetic anthems that speak volumes about her sensitivities and emotions within life itself. Such an excellent masterpiece that needs to be celebrated!"

-Gerry Ellen, *A Big Piece of Driftwood*

More Animal than Human
Mary A. Rogers, 2025
All rights reserved.

Printed in the United States of America.

No part of this book may be used, stored in a system retrieval system, or transmitted, in any form or in any means by electronic, mechanical, photocopying, recording or reproduced in any manner whatsoever without written permission from the publisher, except in the case of brief quotations embodied in critical articles and reviews.

For information, address
Indie Blu(e) Publishing
indieblucollective@gmail.com

Paperback ISBN: 978-1-951724-26-9
eBook ISBN: 978-1-951724-27-6
Library of Congress Control Number: 2024952265
Indie Blu(e) Editorial Team
Candice Louisa Daquin
Victoria Manzi
Christine E. Ray
Elijah R. Carney

Acknowledgments

I want to acknowledge everyone at Indie Blu(e) Publishing that made my dream become a reality. After working with you on the anthologies, *We Will Not Be Silenced*, *But You Don't Look Sick*, and *Through the Looking Glass*, I knew that when it came time to birth my own book of poetry into the world, I only wanted to work with you.

I want to thank the Indie Blu(e) Editorial Team as I appreciate all of you so much: Candice Louisa Daquin, Victoria Manzi, Christine E. Ray, and Elijah R. Carney.

Candice Louisa Daquin, I want to acknowledge you, personally, as you've been an incredible mentor to me. Thank you for all the guidance you've offered along the way. My heart overflows with gratitude.

I would like to thank those who read my words and peered into my soul prior to publication. Thank you for receiving me into your hearts. I am honored.

I would like to thank my family for all of their love and support. To my husband: My handsome. My moon and stars. Without you, none of this would be possible. You are my rock. To my son, KC: I love you. To my sister, Rebecca and my brother, Mark: you mean everything. I love you.

I would like to thank my extended family and in-laws- Vincent, Joanne, and Mary Lyne- along with my aunt, Linda and my uncle, Phil.

I would like to acknowledge Carrie and Evelyn and say thank you. Without you, none of this would have or could have, happened- quite literally.

I love you all so much.

I would like to acknowledge my parents, who have both passed. I wish so many things could have been different, but everything made me who I am. I may be composed of many fragments, but I am whole. I can't help but think you would be proud of the woman I have become and the person I am today. I love you both, eternally. I know that if heaven exists, you're there with my baby- surrounded by all of our ancestors- and animals we've ever loved that have made their way across the rainbow bridge.

Finally, thank you, Dear Reader. Thank you, from the bottom of my heart. Thank you for receiving my words and all the pieces of me.

Dedication

for those I love and those I've lost

and to Corey
you are my heartbeat

Contents

More Animal than Human 1
Immortal 2
The Witching Hour 3
Let the Wolves Run Free 4
Beautiful, Strong, Independent Woman 5
Rise, Darling, Rise 9
La Loba 10
All Hail the Queen 12
A Starless Sea 16
I Do Not Profess 18
Prisms 20
Rage 23
Everything 25
Singing Over the Bones 27
The Sky is Falling 28
Fallen Angel 30
The Phoenix 32
The Dance Before the Tomb 33
Day by Day 34
The Priestess & The Nun 36

The In-Between 38
Grandmother Willow.. 40
Recipe of Love 42
Momma... 47
Unwanted 50
Death Defined by the Living... 52
Grief 54
Death on Replay 56
The Four Winds 58
Samhain.. 59
Natural Disaster 60
The Sky Cries 62
When Love Dies... 64
The Perfect Storm.. 65
The Invitation 67
Embers.. 69
Metamorphosis.. 71
Alone... 73
The First Step 75
Silence... 76
Witch Weather... 79
Honey & Seduction... 81

Nectar	82
Am I Your Muse?	83
Sunrise	85
This Moment	86
Encased Amber	87
The Wild	88
Rapture	89
Seduced by Nature	90
Love	91
This Moment is My Life	92
Lightly	93
Atlas	94
Enchantment	95
Moon After Moon	96
Fireflies & Fairytales	100
The Raven Stole the Moon	102

More Animal than Human

born under the light
of a full pregnant moon
breath and sweat
a savage monsoon

the heavens clapped and rejoiced
tears falling like rain
as the holy mother screamed
and cried out in pain

birthed from the loins
of Gaia's saltwater womb
on the night you were buried
in an ancestral tomb

for you are the phoenix
resurrected from a catacomb of ash
spark of ember, flame of match
one with the ethers and cosmic expanse

god, animal, human— primate sublime
fire, death, resurrection— time after time
not just a god, but an animal too
more animal than human, wild but subdued.

Immortal

destiny was born the day you took your first breath and the seal that bound the book that was to become your life— broke wide open. windswept pages, gilded in gold— hours, days, and weeks gone by. documenting each time you laughed or cried.

a living masterpiece

three parts to this play— but acting would never be your forte, nay. you are an artist. born to be naked— slinging black ink onto pages of white— writing your journey as it unfolds. resuscitating life from shattered bones.

your legacy

when hope was born— you nurtured her, buried her— and then gnawed and clawed at the dirt, time and time again. for immortal is she. breadth and depth. heartbeat and soul.

you called her by another name: life— eternal and everlasting.

The Witching Hour

there is a time of day, when shadows are cast in
twilight— encasing life in amber and gold.

as the sun dips below the horizon, the enchanting moon
takes her place in the night sky— throwing off her
blanket of stars.

while others sleep and dream— i will rise.
for when the witching hour is near, it's time to dance
and sing.

it's time to make mischief with the creatures of the
night.

Let the Wolves Run Free

a cave— hieroglyphic walls
the scent of dried herbs and earth

burnt sage and fire

runes— chicken bones
fur, hide, and blood sacrifice

athame and chalice
obsidian glass

reflection pool
the womb of Gaia

the crone sings over a pile of bones
calling the ancestors home

chanting to the rhythm of the mother drum
heartbeat. pulse. enigma of sound
the crone cries out, *"let the wolves run free"*

and the babe, fresh from the womb
screams
as she takes her first breath

born of darkness and stars
the full moon smiles.

Beautiful, Strong, Independent Woman

you were born
under the light of the moon
to stand tall, resurrected in all your glory
fierce like a mighty oak
with many far-reaching branches
and roots that sink deep
into the rich underbelly of Gaia
you were given wings to fly, to soar
to the tallest peak of the highest mountain
and gills to swim
in the deepest depths of the roaring sea

beautiful, strong, independent woman
you were meant to run fast and free
through rain forests lush and green
jane, swinging from tree to tree
fast as a gazelle; sleek and stealth
an oracle's intuition to trust yourself
azura of the crimson gate—
princess of dusk and dawn
one with the ancestors and gods long gone
yes, dear goddess, to them you belong

beautiful, strong, independent woman
you are truth— uncensored, naked, and raw

More Animal Than Human   Mary A. Rogers

beautiful, strong, independent woman
you were meant to be free
you were meant to run naked across landscapes
without the shackles of time
licking berry stained fingertips
washing down the gift offered from the universe
with crystal clear refreshment melted from snowy peaks
you were meant to be barefoot
digging your toes in the rich green velvet carpet
while inhaling the sweet aroma of honeysuckle and
hyacinth
you were never meant to compromised or silenced
the lies of the serpent brought uncertainty; insecurity

beautiful, strong, independent woman
let your hips sway under the light of the full pregnant
moon
feel the warmth of the whiskey coil through your insides
until you feel the warmth in the center of your
femininity
move your body to the beat and rhythm
drums and tambourines
feel the light of the bonfire move through you
let your love ripple and radiate through the universe

shake your curls free as they cascade and dance around
you
with a rhythm all their own
inhale the scent of cedar and evergreen

More Animal Than Human   Mary A. Rogers

raise your hands to the milky way and let the breeze
move you
welcome your emotions and visions as you would an old
friend
an oracle in a trance: allow it, feel it, and then set it free

beautiful, strong, independent woman
there is a wild woman awakening inside of you
do not suffocate or stifle her
birth her into the universe to shine
under the light of the full pregnant moon
to stand tall, resurrected in all her glory
her divine feminine
fierce like a mighty oak
with many far reaching branches
roots that sink deep into the rich soil of the earth
her spirit was meant to soar as a regal hawk
to fly to the tallest peak of the highest mountain
and to free-fall to the deepest depths of the roaring sea.

More Animal Than Human Mary A. Rogers

Rise, Darling, Rise

a loud gathering
mardi gras in the rain
noise, noise –so much noise
too much noise
the crowd exploded with applause

the curtains parted, as curtains do
a hush, a whisper, a gasp
silence
sweet, sweet quiet of night
a single tear fell but a smile began to rise
tut-tut-tut, rapture came
they came to see a swan transcend
this was no goddess but her Kali friend

from a crumbled state on the floor
the ash gave way as embers burned
she rose, eyes piercing, in holy rage
"are thou not pleased?"
naked, she stood for all to see
her eyes darting across the room
her judge and jury ready to prosecute.

La Loba

somewhere between myth and time, stands a grand and ancient temple where the old one lives.

many have called her witch;
others call her god.

in the inner sanctum of the temple, there is a round room.
a cave of sorts— where sunlight cannot enter.

grand columns have been erected.
stones etched with stories throughout the ages.

a sanctuary lost to the sands of time.

smoke and incense flood the room,
candles flicker— dancing in shadows around the circumference.

soul songs and sacred chants— one sound building upon the other, until there's a faint chorus of symphony.

whispers floating on the wind.

tall, ornate doors— carved from the ancient grandmother trees, follow the curve of the room.

each door guarded by a veiled priestess.

in the center of the room burns a pit of fire,

and there, crawling on the dark earth, is she— sifting through a pile of bones.

as she moves and sways with her hands dancing through the air, the bones begin to take shape and eventually flesh out.

with one primal, guttural sound, the wolf rises from its eternal slumber and begins to howl— before running towards the moon.

All Hail the Queen

a babe
cradled in the woods
nestled between berry and fern

so fresh. so pure
ethereal. wild
raised by raven and wolf

age five
she's still alive
she has survived

huntress. forager
she knows each plant by name
the language she speaks— native to the land

all hail the queen

age fifteen
she longs to be seen
there is a crevice in her heart

touch. kinship. her own kind
a fault-line. waiting to shift
waiting to erupt

More Animal Than Human Mary A. Rogers

her emotions heavy
outcast

age twenty
she's taken to the edge of the forest
here she hides and here she seeks

watcher. voyeur
climbing the tallest of trees
she makes dolls from pine and twig

lines them in a row

family. friend. foe
all eventually succumb to the crow

all hail the queen

forgotten. haunted. ghost
she haunts the forest as a daughter of the night
cloaked in fog— out of sight

time passes, year after year after year
until finally, she's enters the phase of the crone

her heart is no longer heavy
though she's still alone

rejected by society

More Animal Than Human   Mary A. Rogers

abandoned by her family
she didn't live in a castle made of glass
nor a building gilded in gold

instead she lived in the forest
the garden of eden, her paradise
a sacred sanctuary, all her own

all hail the queen.

More Animal Than Human   Mary A. Rogers

A Starless Sea

when i think of my childhood
the words salt and honey
salivate in my mouth— bittersweet

my first memories
fragments of a dream
bottles and dogs and halloween
fear and betrayal
sirens and flashing lights

missing eyebrows
my mother's screams
my father on a gurney
my mother stealing us away

to sleep on church pews
bible study and baby jesus
easy bake ovens and moon pies
robots, cartoons, and make believe

strawberries, sunflowers, and fields of lavender
swing sets and tongue glued to a flagpole
scissors and burps and learning
how to spell my name and count by dots

having my art critiqued
criticized for coloring outside of the lines

More Animal Than Human Mary A. Rogers

being introduced to bullies
and fair-weathered friends

i learned about love and loss
words: divorce and custody
racism and prejudice
stepmother— the wicked kind

followed by years and years
of darkness— deleted files
where memories splinter
polaroids, a quick flash, and then erasure

the reel of my life has lost its focus
few memories remain— while the rest
are chained in darkness
at the bottom of a starless sea.

I Do Not Profess

to be a leader
a teacher, nor a prophet

i am not a god—
though i embraced my inner goddess
centuries ago

i am bent but i'm not broken
i am fragile, but i'm also strong

i am fierce— i am fire
a fucking warrior
and everything in between

i am perfect chaos

my beliefs lie somewhere
between buddhist and baptist

i am contradiction
want and need

i am hungry for truth
i love, i lust, i desire

i am stained glass
light and vibrant color

More Animal Than Human   Mary A. Rogers

i am laughter— i am joy
i am darkness and despair

i have fought fierce battles
slain demons and dragons

because i am life
and i will always overcome.

Prisms

i am a human kaleidoscope
a myriad of colors
shapes and forms
every petal of this flower
singular
yet together, prisms

prisms everywhere

the color of my love
is red. for blood
for heart. for pulse
for my ancestors

the natives. the savages
who held sacred
the majestic purple mountains
and planted the fields
amber waves of grain

the color of my soul
is yellow. for sunflowers
for daisies and forget-me-nots
the history
a war-torn country
tradition and a way of life
a way of being

More Animal Than Human   Mary A. Rogers

wisdom, dignity, and poise

the color of my almond-shaped eyes
are brown. representing soil and earth
growth and roots
for a life of rich exploration
reflection and excavation
an entire galaxy
lives inside of me

my body is a full spectrum
of ink and art and words
hopes and dreams
and so many disappointments
a body that has known
profound love. profound loss
and all the hues of blue

transgressional scars
mapped in marshmallow pink
running in lines across my flesh
tiger stripes, telling a story
of a life my lover reads in braille
a consecrated text
full of constellations
that map the journey
of my heart
the atlas to my soul

every chapter has been bound
just beneath my skin
prefaced and prologued
with the wisdom and stories
of my ancestors. shamans
who revered the ways of old
but how this memoir ends
that alone
will be my own tale to tell

i am a human kaleidoscope
a myriad of colors
shapes and forms
every petal of this flower
singular
yet together, prisms

prisms, everywhere.

Rage

i am the tempest
raging like the roaring sea

a tsunami of fury

i am a hurricane
a volcano ready to erupt

to burn it all down

so that nothing remains
but bone and ash

retribution

i am a caged animal; trapped
ready to gnaw and claw

my way to freedom

brimstone and hellfire
this is more than a revolution

and there will be no white flag
nor surrender

for i am rage, made manifest

More Animal Than Human — Mary A. Rogers

i demand judgment and justice
twelve jurors at my behest

i will have my vengeance
in this life, or the next.

Everything

the fire begins a slow burn
rising from between my thighs
the dragon has awoken

rising. rising

primal serpent
sovereign queen
the flame eroding
bend your knee

rising. rising

from my mouth
i will devour
i will destroy
this fire, this rage

rising. rising

i hear her voice
the voice of she
who will be silenced no more
it is the voice of *i am*

rising. rising

More Animal Than Human   Mary A. Rogers

the wailing of the deep
heart of Gaia
bass of the mother drum
pulse and heartbeat

rising. rising

until like a dying star
i implode— i explode
and for a moment
i am infinite

falling. falling

i am creation
i am death
i am *she*
i am

everything. everything.

Singing Over the Bones

i am in the graveyard
sifting through bones
not to dredge up my past
or even to question my future
i'm simply recovering and collecting
fragmented pieces of my soul.

The Sky is Falling

i danced around the fire
with my ancestors

we prayed for rain
for emotion to descend

the sky is falling

wrapped in the skin of brother bear
and a headdress of feathers

someone beat the mother drum
as we howled the mighty wolf song

touched by the hands
of the gods

the moon smiled
as it devoured the sun

the sky is falling

the stars glimmered
silver herrings

and that night i slept
in the belly of a whale

i touched the edge
of infinity

i wept as i beheld
the ineffable beauty

my tears fed the earth
and i came alive.

Fallen Angel

words. love. lust
unbridled power

music. so much music
and so many wings

sweet nectar of memories

something like silence
and the space in-between

breath and heartbeat

fueled by whisky
and too much caffeine

ash of cigarette
offerings and nicotine

communing
with ancestors of old

in the land of dreams

dancing around galaxies
endless stars of gold

revealing elysian mysteries
centuries, untold

drenched in the blood of gods
flesh of my flesh

to the ancients alone
will i one day atone

initiated into the land of the lost
crowned in the land of plenty

carnal and hedonistic
green eyes of envy

who am i

so many faces have come and gone
some lingering longer than others

flesh, tears, heartbeat. soul
salt and bone

holy whore, made mother
fallen angel, turned crone.

The Phoenix

she loved wings and sky and wide-open spaces. passion and play and erotic seduction. her hips would sway and love under the light of the moon.

to know her was to understand the ocean: vast beautiful, uncharted depth.

poseidon's chaos and calypso's kiss.
and yet, she was also pure, like spring rain.

she yearned to break free— of her thoughts, her own self judgment, her pain.

one day, i watched as she stood atop a mountain—hurling rocks while hurling words. all the words that stung, that stuck— about who she was, who she wasn't, who she should be, or who she needed to become.

words caught on the wind: worthless, unlovable, nothing.

and i watched her transform.

her eyes lit with desire and feather by feather— she grew wings and caught fire. everything around her burned— her past, the present, her future. a lifetime in flames.

haunted ghosts rising.

The Dance Before the Tomb

i'm dreaming of the wild, freedom, and the dance before the tomb. fresh, honey crisp air, i will drink the sun and feast on the moon.

i will live at the edge of the world, surrounded by forest and stream. i will follow my dreams through a forest of pine; tree by sacred tree.

i will write at a wooden desk— carved and sacrificed for me. i will grow my food and fresh nectar— honey from the bees.

i will have shelves full of books. notebooks lined with poetry and prose. memories and dreams— my life planted in perfect little rows.

there will be herbs drying from the rafters and a hearth full of wax. i will forage for nuts and berries— and carry a bow when following tracks.

i will bathe in the river and drink from the stream. i will be one with nature. my soul will be redeemed.

Day by Day

there are days i crave and yearn for his touch

there are days it feels as though he's taken complete residence
within my heart and has seen all the colors of my soul

there are days i take refuge in his strong embrace
and lose myself in the essence of his being

there are days i feel disconnected
from everything and everyone

in nature, i often find myself lost
on a trail in the middle of nowhere

there are days i am sad
and consumed with heart wrenching grief

these are the days i long to lie my head in my mother's lap
where she plays with the curl at the nape of my neck
as she once did when she was alive

there are the days i long to hold
the babe that once grew and died within my womb

and these are the hardest days of all—

More Animal Than Human — Mary A. Rogers

as they bring me to the precipice of despair

these are the days i can be found
hugging my knees on the floor of the shower

where hot water and tears become one

but my favorite days
are the days when i feel strong
powerful for all i have overcome

these are the days i cherish most—

these particular days
find me surrounded by beautiful souls
hearty food, and much needed laughter

these are the days the sun shines bright
and my smile lights the universe

across the blackness of night
i am a star shining
amongst so many others in the milky way

these are the days i wish would last forever.

The Priestess & The Nun

inside me live two women— they have been there for as long as i can recall. i don't know when my soul fractured/fragmented, or if that's the case at all.

it is the dualistic nature of she. the devil and angel on opposing sides.

the priestess knows the light but prefers to work in the dark. she is medicine, mystic, sage, and wild woman. it is she who runs with the wolves, howls with the moon, and dances in the forest after dark.

she is catacombs, prisms, cypress, and spells. it is she that knows me and i find freedom in her embrace.

the nun is righteous, holy indignation, and saint. it is she who holds the reins most of the time. she is love, compassion, and judgment in one.

she tells me good from bad and right from wrong. she strokes my hair while whispering of purgatory and hell. it is she who taught me of guilt, shame, penance, and mortification of the flesh.

somewhere in the midst of this chaos of opposing forces— i've decided to integrate. and it feels like death and destruction.

the war has not yet been won.

but my heart has been weighed against the feather and i am coming home.

The In-Between

i'm thinking of wide-open spaces
of choice, acceptance, and grief
how often my thoughts go concave
reaching deep into the darkness
for stillness, comfort, and release

and how forest, wild, and ocean
moss, moon, and stars
have the power to resuscitate my soul

i'm thinking of all the little things
how they add up to become all the things
the everything's
and how it's not always something
that can be pointed to and named

i'm thinking of the love affair
between the sun and moon
twilight, sunrise, and eclipse
the moment when two
suddenly become one

i'm thinking of moonlit vistas
and ancient prophecies
about rock and wave
and how i come alive

More Animal Than Human Mary A. Rogers

like a horse unbridled— untamed
mounting the sea and riding the tide

i'm thinking of hope, want, and desire
feelings and feral need
birds and ancestral whispers
hushed poetry dancing through the trees

and what it is to have a heart
beating through ribs of cage
of wings and flight, life and death
and everything in-between.

Grandmother Willow

the ancient and wise grandmother willow, a legendary oracle beckoned, "*come to me, dear child, and tell me what is the matter. come now, go on...*"

i snuggled into her roots as a child would on her mother's lap.

"*i am hurting,*" i replied. "*my body has been holding too much grief and too much pain. i can't seem to just let it all go.*"

"*come now, child. hug me,*" she instructed.

i stretched my arms wide around her trunk - my cheek upon her bark.

she and i seemed to weep in unison as her branches danced upon the wind.

i kept my eyes closed and i could feel the pain leaving my body— being replaced with comfort and warmth— reassurance and love.

feeling restored from the transference, i pulled away but found that her leaves— once vibrant and green— had turned to autumn.

one by one, they fell to the ground.

"*grandmother, what have I done*?!" i cried out in despair.

smiling a tired smile, she simply replied, "*oh no. hush now, child. to everything there is a season, and a time to every purpose under the heaven: a time to be born, a time to die. a time to plant, and a time to harvest...*"

as she continued, i found myself reciting ecclesiastes 3 with her— until at last, the final leaf fell and grandmother willow closed her tired eyes, forever.

Recipe of Love

she rose
while it was still dark outside
while the rest of the house
exhaled soft breaths of slumber
only the dogs stirred
following her steps
the *pitter patter* of paws
and the *click, click, click*
of their nails on the hardwood floors

she begins the day
by starting a fire in the hearth
the warmth ignites
from the embers of her love
she starts the coffee press
and places a kettle of water
on the rusted wood stove

she pulls on her sweater
rubber boots over sweatpants
the creaky screen door
slamming shut behind her
as the dogs run on ahead
and a song begins in her heart

she hums as she walks
tasting the gospel on her lips

More Animal Than Human 　　　　　　　　Mary A. Rogers

she spreads the feed
and collects the eggs
turns on the hose
filling troughs and water bowls

she returns to the kitchen
every move followed
by watchful canines
she fills their bowls
before pulling out the risen dough
spreads flour on the counter
and begins to roll and knead and stretch
in the same way that others
often stretch the truth

she pulls out the cast iron skillet
turning down the heat
when the bacon began to hiss and spit
she transfers the cooked fat
preparing to make country gravy
a recipe passed down
generation to generation,
as this is the first time
in a long time
multiple generations are sleeping
under the same roof

as she begins to sprinkle this
with a few pinches of that

More Animal Than Human   Mary A. Rogers

she thinks of the generations
that went before her
all of them now passed
she is now the matriarch
the wise woman with so much wisdom to share
while her grandchildren's only interests
seem to live in the television
on their phones or computer screens

her cooking, the family's saving grace
as they would now gather
to share
to eat
to love
to argue
to play
to pray

but who will be the glue
once she is put to pasture?

one of the dogs whimpered
pulling her from her thoughts
the child appears
eyes glistening, half asleep
hair wild, wearing pajamas
the ones with the sewed in feet
one by one, the family gently rises
gathering around the kitchen

gathering in the heart of the home
as everyone plans their day,
she knows what she must do

yule comes early that year
as she has fallen ill
the family comes together
each vying to work their hands
the way that grief works their hearts
one starts a fire
another, the coffee press
one goes out to feed
while another tends to the hounds
lined along the counter
they find a gift wrapped for each one
inside is a handwritten cookbook
recipes passed
from generation to generation
filled with pictures and written memories
ancestors, poems, and all the wisdom
she has wanted to share
and so it is
that the family begins to cook
a meal prepared by them all

excited voices ring in chorus
and lying in the bed upstairs
she knows

that while the gravy was probably lumpy
and biscuits likely not cooked all the way through
she smiles in her heart
confident she has done all that she could
and with her final breath, full of love
she drifts away in a state of gratitude.

Momma

their words hit me
like cement being poured

she's taken a turn for the worse
sinking. sinking

the floor beneath me
quicksand

all night
we stayed by your side

all your little ducklings
sitting in a row

the only sound
beeping. beeping

and a tube
forcing you to breathe

my broken heart
willing you to stay alive

i read you a poem
i sang you a song

across the screen
and all space and time

the numbers fell to zero
flatlined

and time stood still

i sat there
for a very long time

empty space
hollow void

i felt my heart
break in two

as primal wails
escaped my lips

my grief was not silent
nor were my apologies

i can't rewind
or turn back time

there will be no forgiveness
and i can't make amends
for this was the final scene

More Animal Than Human Mary A. Rogers

this was the end

guilt and grief
my kryptonite

an abandoned basin
full of tears

my heart aches
a vacant echo

ten years have passed
and i'm forever haunted, still.

Unwanted

it's a feeling i'd had
for as long as i can remember

i blamed my mother
for abandoning me
i had just turned seven

and then one day
my dad was sitting at his desk
i was at the kitchen table

he was typing a bid
i was doing homework

somewhere, out of nowhere, he said

"we didn't want you
i didn't want you
you were a surprise

your mother had an affair
i didn't know if you were mine
i didn't want you"

outcast
orphan
confused

why would he tell me this
when he had once been an orphan too?

i grew up begging for his attention
to hear him once say, he was proud

but those words never came
disappointment

i never lived up to his expectations
and the truth is— i never even tried

strangers

he never understood me
and the truth is— he never made an attempt

even as death kissed his lips

i told people we made amends
a lie i desperately wanted to believe

when he took his last breath
i sobbed as i only ever wanted
to be loved

instead, i was left with the words—
unwanted, still.

Death Defined by the Living
an impression marked by depression

round and round we go

floating on a planet
revolving around the sun
where day always turns to night
and back to day once more

rubber and metal
glide the asphalt river
to and fro

the same schedule
the same, endless rerun
and no one seems to notice

day after day after day

they do it with a smile
and pleasure in their eyes
they dream while awake
living only in their dreams

sometimes there's discontent
unrest, unease
once medically anesthetized
they return to the revolving door

seasons go by

month after month after month

why does no one notice
or feel the death
of endless repetition

words wind themselves
around my heart and through my soul
"what's the point?!"
existential angst

year after year after year

what i hope to leave behind
footprints of a legacy
a legend, reborn
my words, my work— my saving grace

and so i write
to quell meaningless monotony
for not just in my dreams
am i am fully awake, fully aware
and to this i cling, with clenched fists

moment by moment by moment.

Grief

there was a lunar eclipse this morning
and i felt the earth mimic my sorrow
amidst the stillness and the hush—
a vast void, no promise of the morrow

where does the soul go
when the body has turned to dust
where is this god in the heavens
who let time crumble and rust?

where do i go for comfort
when my soul is fraught with woe
for i've learned that out in nature
even the trees must learn to let go

depression has become a corset
bound too tight, i can scarcely breathe
this anguish, a weight too heavy
i'm suffocating from the grief

in a dark river of sadness
i fear i'll one day drown
heavy is the heart that's broken
of one who's buried the crown

this grief feels like a mountain
my shattered heart, unable to bear

someone once told me, that loss
is a pain that's meant to be shared

but i fear if i unleash this darkness
the sun will rise no more
though we now dance with the living
we'll each, one day
be knocking at death's door.

Death on Replay

in the end
we all die

from a broken heart
or a broken body

grief is a well
from which we all must drink

as the wheel of time
turns and turns

one by one
we'll each be summoned

to break the heart
of someone else

i reach my hand back
to reach for my mother

as she once reached for hers

there's a light
at the end of the tunnel

More Animal Than Human   Mary A. Rogers

i'm being expelled
from my mother's womb

i gasp for breath
and scream in horror

as the wheel of time
turns and turns.

The Four Winds

i felt the santa ana winds
warm against my face—
porcelain skin, rouge cheeks
flushed aglow with love

the wind, now razor sharp
wailing through the trees
and i can feel nothing
but haunted memories
and shattered dreams

the wind siphons
and i am trapped
somewhere in the center
where the four winds collide.

Samhain

there's a mystery in the in-between
a shedding of skin and the letting go
the veils have lifted on this eve
a seance that began long ago

on this night, the realms do wander
resurrection in wings aflutter
for in the wild
the ancients do roam

black dog rabid
fangs of white
there was a dead bird flying
through a broken sky

nothing is real
an elaborate illusion
their weary souls
demand absolution

from the delusion
collusion
confusion

branch of white, black of dead
blood lust wolf dressed in red
primal the heart calling ancestor's home
feral is the one who sings over the bones.

Natural Disaster

i am water
i've learned to float; to flow

the temperament of a woman
oh, how quickly it can change

the sea is unforgiving
maybe i am too

i've scorched fire with fire
and watched the whole world burn

i've drowned in the river styx
reborn on a bed of ash

and in my death
i learned that water
is just as powerful as flames

both have the power to heal
both have the power to destroy

guilt often follows incineration
tears flood— a tsunami
quelling the embers

More Animal Than Human   Mary A. Rogers

until i am left standing
alone, in the cracks of my own fault line

i am a dark night and a hurricane.

The Sky Cries

i heard the pitter-patter
of rain dropping
on the canvas umbrella
humming to its own beat
as the earth received

a drink for the tired and weary
something like nourishment
for the soul. the cracks
where a river runs through it
even weeds are encouraged to grow

and it made me think
of love. of loss. of grief
and all the ways it can split
the human heart in two.
how it feels
like time should cease
and how life will defiantly refuse

i looked out the window
the roses bowed their heads
in reverence, in prayer
refusing to meet my gaze
baptized by rolling clouds
and misty skies of gray

More Animal Than Human   Mary A. Rogers

and then i saw a single rose
peeking through her petals
and to my surprise
she met my eyes
willing me to see
music notes on the wind
moving to the beat
primal cries & lullabies
bird songs
a steady hum of wings

my soul
drenched in gratitude
i felt my heart
expand and bloom
the storm i felt
mirrored outside
and in that moment
sparks began to fly
a clap of thunder
lightning strikes

i beckoned to all of the roses
open your eyes, open your eyes
there's comfort in knowing
that sometimes, even the sky cries.

When Love Dies

it begins with a hairline fracture
a break that can't be reset
it grows wider, slowly over time

the great divide

walls have been erected
no bridges left to cross
we've become perfect strangers

wandering the land of the lost

does wisdom say it's worth it?
black hold; heart bled
vengeance or grace, gods willing

depends on which wolf was fed.

The Perfect Storm

i often talk about loneliness
as though it's a self-inflicted wound
but the truth is, i love my solitude
and i only feel lonely
when i'm with you

your eyes
which used to hold a sea of dreams
lit from a lifetime of laughter
are hollow and vacant now

i try to catch a glimpse of your soul
and sometimes, i even think i do

and when i sense you there
my heart emits a soft amber glow
i allow you in. i lay down my shield
unaware you came ready to battle
as i lie bleeding in your arms

empty— an abandoned home
where memories chip
like paint under the heat of the sun
cobwebs and grandfather clock
ticking, ticking, ticking

More Animal Than Human   Mary A. Rogers

ready to stop
and mark the time of death

dying. dying, dying

a body— where i once found refuge
a place to cocoon on the darkest of days
became a body of harm
a body that made me question my own

i hear the crack of the can
and my body folds in on itself
contraction. fear
fermented hops and yeast
and violence

have you ever played
russian roulette
with an addict?

i read some words
narcissist [you]
empath [me]
and i'm drowning in the center
lost in the eye
of a perfect storm.

The Invitation

i want to know who you are
when all of your titles are stripped away

i want to know what fire forged you
into the person you are today

i want to know who you were
before you were told what and who to be

i want to know who you were
when you were still wild, feral, and free

what makes your heart bleed
and sets your soul on fire?

what are your longings
hopes, prayers, and desires?

i don't want a persona
the masks you wear to hide

i want to know your passions
and all that brings you pride

i want to know what makes you happy
what you fear and what makes you cry

reveal to me your truths
everything you are inside

i didn't come to dine with your ego
i came to feast with your soul.

Embers

the morning light glows different—
dimmer somehow
orange dark clouds and sun
casting shadows on everything

and all i love is gone

the ash of memories
of living things
apocalyptic snow
sentient beings
fear and fleeing

and all i love is gone

did the trees cry out
as tongues of fire
ravaged their sacred bones?
vengeance and victory
no borders where she roams

and all i love is gone

the aftermath, quiet and still
hushed cinders and broken heart
determination and will

hungry ghosts do cry out
my spirit remains here still

and all i love lives on.

Metamorphosis

i warned you
be gentle— handle with care
i told you i'm fragile— but worth it
crystal prisms everywhere

did i finish my sentence
before i fell?— nine circles of hell
and shattered
into a million little pieces

and you laughed
you laughed

i stared at you
a million eyes
a million prisms

& my heart stopped beating
stopped bleeding
stopped needing

flatlined
haunted
undone

and then i became
something else

someone else

and i flitted out the window
into the open breeze.

Alone

tonight, i sat in a nook
trying to read
but instead, stared aimlessly
out the window

a storm broke out
lightning crackled
thunder roared
and the sky began to cry

her tears falling
rolling down the glass
to the pitter patter rhythm
of my own pain

i saw myself in a drop
a single drop that became many
and i pondered the power
in the rise and fall of togetherness

droplets joined hands
and dove into a puddle
a divot in the pavement
no beginning and no end

and i wondered how it could be
that in a sea of faces

More Animal Than Human   Mary A. Rogers

one drop could still feel separate
and so very alone.

The First Step

screaming. screaming. screaming
all is silent and no one can hear
drowning. drowning. drowning
no one can see as the water is clear

for this body of mine
has been programmed
to tell a thousand lies
over a thousand years

my heart is hurting
shredded. hemorrhaging
and yet, it continues to beat
so i continue to smile
rather than express and acknowledge
my own damnation and defeat

"*step here,*" they say
"*we promise, it's solid ground*"
shakily, i take one step forward
quicksand— down, down, down
i pull myself up and out
gripping the rocks behind the ledge
white knuckled and short of breath

the first step is the hardest
and it feels something like death.

Silence

sometimes words come
many times they don't
most days are spent in silence
which doesn't mean
the absence of sound
for i'm often surrounded
by laughter in moonbeams

and the orchestra of the forest

it's the ache of yearning
that renders me speechless
the void of voice
imagination and octave
the spine of an oak
raising bare branches
standing at the pulpit
sacrilege

and the spark of desire

the vibrato of soul
slain in politics
fear building through truth
dancing marionettes

More Animal Than Human   Mary A. Rogers

i will the chorus
of the oppressed
rise

but they remain silenced

sometimes words come
many times they don't
which doesn't mean
the absence of sound
for i am surrounded
by mockingbirds
and echo chambers

voices buried
beneath hallowed ground

the sound of my heart
beating. bleeding
wings of thunder
screaming. screeching
tsunami of emotion
madness, teetering
unbridled desire
fleeting. fleeing

until my pen drops

More Animal Than Human   Mary A. Rogers

sometimes words come
many times they don't
most days are spent in silence
which doesn't mean
the absence of sound
for i am surrounded
by animal and ancestor
which is to say
chants and prayers

hope rising. resurrection

and i am reminded
through pulse & heartbeat
pounding through ribs of cage
this breath. this desire
fierce and ferocious
the wolf calling to the moon
i will bleed in ink
to give voice to all.

Witch Weather

the pulse
the static
the stillness

haze and heat
late afternoon dusk

the fire clouds cast their own shadows
as fierce wind creates its own vortex

it's apocalyptic

no filter
pure magic.

Honey & Seduction

imagine, if you will,
a romantic evening in—
nina simone on vinyl
a white bear skin rug
conveniently placed
by the hearth of the fire.

pillows and warm throws,
a crackling amber glow.
you, sipping gamay noir
while your lover recites poetry;
honey and seduction.

Nectar

i want to taste of your flesh
and drink from your veins
the holy sacrament that is you.

to wade in a scrying pool of wonder
ravishing your soul until i
have devoured and explored
every last piece of you.

you're nectar
immortal.
my own personal
fountain of youth.

Am I Your Muse?

in this dark and seedy place
where you recite words
written by giants— the literary greats

i take in your sultry, masculine voice
taste and savor your words
let them roll over my tongue
and through my lips
the richest delicacy

tasting the stars and cursing the moon

filled with longing, i need to know
is this love, lust, or something in between
my soul spews the profanities of my aching heart
through ink onto perfectly lined pages

what is my truth? what is yours?
are you willing to open yourself to me
get naked on paper and bare your soul?
will you invite me to witness that which you hold sacred?
secrets that tear at your insides
that which stirs you awake and haunts you through the night?

More Animal Than Human
Mary A. Rogers

questions remain unanswered
as passion moves us, driving us to your darkened lair
a star that has collapsed within itself
where light has been eclipsed— forever burned out
returned to the black nothingness of the night
my love, if only for tonight—
tell me the words i long to hear

recite to me words written long ago
written by giants— the literary greats
i will take in your sultry, masculine voice
taste and savor your words
let them roll over my tongue
and through my lips
the richest delicacy
tasting the stars and cursing the moon-
for tonight, tonight i am not just your muse
in this dark and seedy place.

Sunrise

there is a blanket of fog winding
through a grove of trees
dancing like a maiden
on a midsummer night's eve

starlight has faded
the moon, barely aglow
the sun peaks over the horizon
as njord blasts a mighty blow

the fog billows and sways
a pirouette, pas de deux
the trees are willing lovers
desire dressed in morning dew

the sun continues rising
casting a fiery, golden spell
enchanting the dream of morning
kissing the moon and fog farewell.

This Moment

gods and ghosts may write my history
oracles may foresee my future
the fates may predict my destiny
but now— right now
this moment, belongs wholly to me

Encased Amber

i am part stars, part sun
daughter of the moon

i am meadow and wildflower
tree and earth and encased amber

i am roots and wings
(so many wings)

and i share a heartbeat
with the creatures of the wild.

The Wild

my soul is out there
somewhere in the wild
roaming through the forest
and communing with the moon.

Rapture

passion in movement
the rhythm and the beat

bass pulsing
primal release

i am fire; i am flame
i've lost control

feral and wild
i let myself go

my ancestors dance with me
and i've never felt more alive

wild, wild nights.

Seduced by Nature

i met nature in the wild and we've been having a glorious love affair ever since. sometimes my soul feels fractured— but she always makes me whole.

she romances me with gifts— feather upon feather, seashell, wood, rock, moss, and stone. trees that sing as the wind takes sail. wildflowers painted amidst cotton candy skies. raindrops and lullabies. birdsongs and symphony. sunshine hugs and seafoam kisses.

she shields me with her concave forest— so that i may laugh, or cry, or scream. she cloaks me in darkness, held by the constellations of the night sky— so that i may howl, long into the night of my despair.

she taught me to be vulnerable— to learn to let go— as the seasons change and the trees strip naked every fall. she introduced me to the moon to learn how my soul may wax or wane. she introduced me to the stars to see that it is in the deepest darkness that i carry the greatest spark. she introduced me to the sun so that i may know that even on the longest night, the sun will always rise once more.

Love

i am in love with words
stories and people
how some can articulate what i cannot

those who can resuscitate life and breath
to make even the most mundane
feel magical and profound
like an adventure

i believe in love beyond differences
beyond opinions and belief
i love the curious— the seekers
those who dive into the waters deep

those who make living and life
feel like poetry and prose
i love swimming in their words
aquatic helium for the soul.

This Moment is My Life

today i cried while gazing at a wildflower
overwhelmed by its beauty and grace
i stared amidst a forest concealed but free
pine, oak, juniper; an array of shades and hue
overhead i watched four vultures in flight
black wings spread amidst clouds of white
i heard my name called upon the wind
before the gentle breeze sweetly kissed my cheek
i inhaled deeply all this beauty beholden to none
i stretched my neck towards the heavens
for this life is vast beautiful
and i am forever grateful in this moment
for this moment is my life.

Lightly

i will walk lightly upon the earth
unafraid and undisturbed
communing with nature
listening to the wisdom
whispered through the leaves
engraved upon my heart
etched upon my soul

the trees
the roots
the water

and so many wings.

Atlas

my love flows ocean deep and can be counted by the infinite stars amidst the galaxy.

i have entire constellations mapped across my heart— an atlas for those curious enough to wander— and the north star, to always carry me home.

for i hold multitudes within my soul.

Enchantment

my soul is enchanted
by the twilight of dawn
when the cicada's hush
and the birds
welcome in a new morning
in song, in prayer, in mating calls
when the stars are aglow
and the moon slowly fades
as the sun
peaks over the horizon
batting her lashes of warmth
across the cool and frosty land.

Moon After Moon

life, ever changing
energy, transformed
these are the words
nature carved
deep into the bark
of my soul

the way a tree
green bright in the spring
moves through the rainbow
as the earth orbits the sun
until winter
makes her grand appearance
blanketing everything
in snow-white innocence
she arrives, crystalized

stripping the tree
of every last leaf
leaving her raw
vulnerable and exposed
i run my fingers down her spine
through her secrets
and over her bones
i ask her to tell me
if anything ever remains the same

More Animal Than Human   Mary A. Rogers

i think of my mother
my father, my child
and how even their footprints
have been covered
by the blizzards of time
how i can't rewind
as life continues, ever forward

i think about how
truth is subjective— selective
how belief is born from perspective
memories— reflective
and how beauty is objective

until i finally conclude
what doesn't change
is the inevitable fact
that everything
eventually will

love and memories and hope
i believe these can live
through lifetimes
and yet, immortality
is gifted to none

i stand with arms wrapped
around the body of the tree
tears falling like rain

More Animal Than Human   Mary A. Rogers

please tell me, oh ancient one
does anything ever
remain the same?

dogs will always bark
as wolves howl & horses bray
and the longing in your heart
will never, ever go away
but know that as the crow flies
love like energy
can never really die

just as every living thing
needs to breathe
so too, will the trees
regrow their leaves

the cycle of life
never changes
but you can embrace
all the meaningful exchanges
you can run towards love
and outrun fear

and rest your mind
as some things do stay
through your ancestral blood
climbing the ladder of your dna

life, ever changing
energy, transformed
these are the words
nature carved
deep into the bark of my soul

moon after moon after moon.

Fireflies & Fairytales

I want to live on the edge of the world surrounded by forest and streams. I will foretell fortunes with the throwing of runes— carved bone harvested from the forest floor. I will write poetry and novels from a nook in a cave before napping with the wolves. I will brew elderberry syrup as arnica oil rests on the windowsill, alongside homemade apple pie. There will be herbs and flowers from foraging hanging from the rafters— lavender and sage.

I will forage and introduce myself to the woods— greeting each plant and herb and tree by name. I will sew white curtains while drinking tea from a cup of stars. The only sounds will be from the woods and the daily whistle of the kettle scattered somewhere between water, windchimes, and the song of my soul sung in harmony with the birds and the trees.

I will spend my spring clearing and planting neat little rows. Fall will bring the harvest and I will have a cellar full of mason jars— brimming with the bounty of summer. I will make strawberry and plum jam to eat with clotted cream on biscuits rolled and patted with flour— baked a perfect golden brown. I will splurge on peach cobbler with blackberry-stained fingertips.

My home will smell of plants and earth and freshly baked cookies. I will bathe in the streams under the light of the moon. I will dance in open fields with the fireflies, fairies, and sprites. I will wander with the guidance of raven and hawk. I will stop to rest in meadows basking in wildflowers. I will collect and chop wood and I will commune daily with the ancestors. I will light candles and hearth while making crown wreaths full of baby's breath, acorns, sunflowers, and leaves. And I shall forever dream under the stars illuminating the milky way.

This poem was originally published in 2021 by the University of Tampa Press: Tampa Review Literary Journal, Issue 61/62. Distributed online to their Education Department.

The Raven Stole the Moon

may you always dance with fairies
catching stars while running with the wolves
fairytales and fireflies
the raven steals the moon.

About the Author

Mary A. Rogers is a poet, writer, and story collector. She has been published in several online publications as well as being a contributing writer to three anthologies published by Indie Blu(e) Publishing: *We Will Not Be Silenced: The Lived Experience of Sexual Harassment and Sexual Assault Told Powerfully Through Poetry, Prose, Essay, and Art*, *Through The Looking Glass: Reflecting on Madness and Chaos Within*, and *But You Don't Look Sick: The Real Life Adventures of Fibro Bitches, Lupus Warriors, and other Superheroes Battling Invisible Illness*.

Her writings have also been featured in *Elephant Journal, Gathering Stories, House of Citrine, Huffington Post, Idaho Magazine, Medium, The OC87 Recovery Diaries, Tampa Review* (61/62), *The Tattooed Buddha,* and *The Urban Howl.*

She is the Founder and Host of the podcast, *Narrative*, which is available on all podcast streaming platforms. Ms. Rogers became fascinated, at a very young age, with comparative mythology and religion. She spent a great portion of her life thus far researching histories, cultures, mythologies, traditions, and religions in order to weave together many tales and ancestral stories- a tapestry of a collective and cohesive history that spans lifetimes.

Having a challenging childhood, Ms. Rogers would often escape into books as a form of distraction. As she got older, she fell in love with reading other people's journals and began keeping her own journals as a way to write down and manage her thoughts and feelings.

Later, she received several books of poetry written by Sylvia Plath and began writing poetry herself. She loved the emotion it invoked while remaining an abstract medium- a means to process her feelings without oversharing or revealing too much. Writing became her therapy.

After enduring a four-year period in which she lost most of her family (both parents, a baby, her last remaining grandparent) and struggling with her health (both physical and mental), writing became the only balm that could soothe her soul; the medicine to mend her broken heart.

Ms. Rogers had a sixteen-year career in healthcare working in administration and management. She went on to become a certified and accredited life coach, reiki master, and sound healer. It became her life passion to help others claw their way back from whatever abyss had consumed them.

She continued this work for several years while working at a yoga/meditation center, until her health would no longer allow it. Deemed permanently disabled, Ms. Rogers moved to a cabin, tucked away in the woods, where she is currently residing.

As a verified Native (Apsáalooke/Crow) and Korean (her father was born in Seoul), her walk in this life is very close to the land and all that inhabits the wild.

While she has many passions, including gardening and sourdough, her greatest passion will always be getting naked on paper.

Artwork Credits

Front Cover: Salo Gwyn, Shutterstock
'The Witching Hour' (page 3): Anastasiia Lakusheva
'Beautiful, Strong, Independent Woman' (page 8): Ank Design
'La Loba' (page 11): Natalia Baginska
'All Hail the Queen' (page 15): Mara Sprier
'I Do Not Profess' (page 19): Valentina Khomutova
'Rage' (page 24): Chainat Prachatree
'Singing Over the Bones' (page 27): Dreya Novak
'The Sky is Falling' (page 29): Natalia Churzina
'The Priestess and the Nun' (page 37): Наталья Шемелина
'The In-Between' (page 39): Creativedesign49
'Grandmother Willow' (page 41): Ank Design
'Recipe of Love' (page 46): Anastasia Sergienko
'Grief' (page 55): Maria Kuznetsova
'Death On Replay' (page 57): Kateryna Kovarzh
'The Four Winds' (page 58): Dreya Novak
'Natural Disaster' (page 61): Nanne Tiggelman
'The Invitation' (page 68): Creativedesign49
'Embers' (page 70): DIY Team
'Metamorphosis' (page 72): Quirkjunkjournals
'Alone' (page 74): Maria Voinova
'Witch Weather' (page 80): Ilona Shorokhova
'This Moment' (page 86): Elena Bessonova
'Encased Amber' (page 97): Ractapopulous
'The Wild' (page 88): Juliia Tochilina

'This Moment Is My Life' (page 92): Ola Tarakanova
'Lightly' (page 93): Cyvv
'Atlas' (page 94): Kateryna Kovarzh
'Enchantment' (page 95): Eglė Lipeikaitė
'Moon After Moon' (page 99): Anne-Marie Ridderhof
'Fireflies and Fairytales' (page 101): Lazarosv
'The Raven Stole the Moon' (page 102): Juliia Tochilina

Other Indie Blu(e) Publishing Titles You Might Enjoy

WE WILL NOT BE SILENCED

The Lived Experience of Sexual Harassment and Sexual Assault Told Powerfully Through Poetry, Prose, Essay, and Art

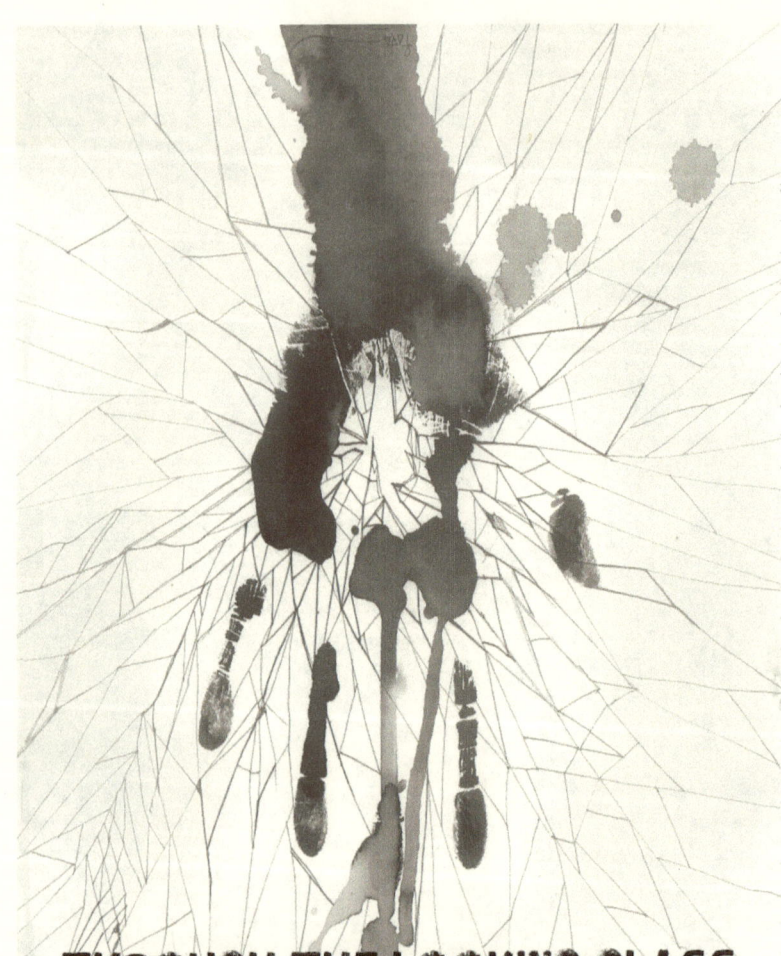

SEASON OF THE SORCERESS

MELODY LEE
Author of the Bestselling Moon Gypsy

Indie Blu(e) Publishing is a progressive, feminist micro-press, committed to producing honest and thought-provoking works. Our anthologies are meant to celebrate diversity and raise awareness. The editors all passionately advocate for human rights; mental health awareness; chronic illness awareness; sexual abuse survivors; and LGBTQ+ equality. It is our mission, and a great honor, to provide platforms for those voices that are stifled and stigmatized.

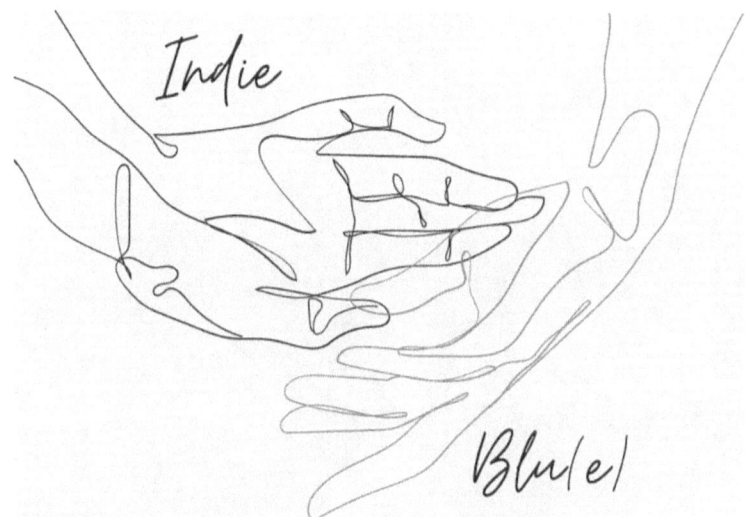

Indie Blu(e) Publishing wants your best and most incisive work. We are welcoming to all artists/writers regardless of race, orientation, gender, gender expression/identity, body type, ability, religious beliefs, income, or immigration status. We are actively seeking submissions from under-represented voices, including artists/authors who are Black, Brown, women, indigenous, gender-nonconforming, people with disabilities, lgbtqia+, and neurodivergent.

We will not accept/publish pieces that depict gratuitous violence, racism, sexism, homophobia, transphobia, xenophobia, and/or hate speech.

www.ingramcontent.com/pod-product-compliance
Lightning Source LLC
Chambersburg PA
CBHW060530080526
44586CB00012B/686